Original title:
Ripples in the Depths

Copyright © 2025 Creative Arts Management OÜ
All rights reserved.

Author: Gideon Shaw
ISBN HARDBACK: 978-1-80587-425-6
ISBN PAPERBACK: 978-1-80587-895-7

Murmurs from the Depths

In the pond, a frog does croak,
He tells the fish the silliest joke.
A turtle chuckles, a gaffe so grand,
As splashes fly from a waterlogged hand.

The catfish giggles in bubbles of glee,
'What's the best way to catch a bee?'
The goldfish grins with a knowing wink,
'Just don't let 'em catch you at the sink!'

Tides of Uncharted Thoughts

Waves of ideas, all swimming around,
Like ducks on a pond, they don't make a sound.
Then one jumps up with a splash and a flap,
'I just remembered, I forgot my map!'

The currents swirl, as the fish start to plot,
'What if we swim to that big crowded spot?'
They gather their courage, then give a great cheer,
A fish on a quest to face all their fear!

The Still Water's Song

Calm waters shimmer, reflecting the sky,
But who made the waves? We're all wondering why.
A duck paddles by with a quack and a sway,
'You'd think with this calm, I would get to play!'

A splash from below, might be a big fish,
But it turns out to be… just my last dish!
The meal that I dropped, now dances around,
In this still, quiet world, chaos is found.

Reflections in Twilight's Embrace

At dusk, the twilight begins to unfold,
Fish telling stories, all silent yet bold.
A shadow appears, it's a cat with big dreams,
Learning to fish, or so it still seems.

The water whispers, a chuckle so light,
As the cat uses bait made of yarn so bright.
'Let's see who's hungry!' It shouts with a grin,
While the fish laugh aloud, 'Oh, where to begin?'

Chasms of Unvoiced Thoughts

In the empty corners, thoughts sit tight,
Like cats in boxes, some take flight.
They munch on silence, sipping tea,
Wondering if they ever would be free.

A pondered joke in the air so stark,
Does a whisper giggle in the dark?
These thoughts remain just out of reach,
Like hidden shells on a sandy beach.

The Fluidity of Forgotten Paths

A pathway rolls like a slip-n-slide,
With memories giggling, trying to hide.
They trip on laughter, slip on cheer,
Dancing with shadows, awfully near.

Lost socks wander down the lane,
Playing tag with stubborn rain.
If only they could find the door,
To join the mayhem of the floor.

Whispers Beneath the Surface

Shh... listen close, there's chatter low,
Where jokes and jests all come to flow.
The depths can be a silly place,
Where jokes play hide and seek with grace.

A fish just winked, it found the right hook,
Diving for laughs in its little nook.
Bubbles giggle, rising with glee,
Telling tales, oh fishy spree!

Echoes of the Abyss

Down in the deep, echoes bounce and play,
Making fun of fish who've lost their way.
A timid shark with a ticklish fin,
Squeals at the bubbles; oh, let the fun begin!

A chorus of giggles, a wave of sound,
As the bottom muck joins in, profound.
What jokes they tell in the ocean's bed,
Where even the sea cucumbers crack a thread!

Beneath the Calm

In waters clear, the fish do dance,
A lobster wearing shades takes a chance.
A clam starts humming a silly tune,
While jellyfish wobble, quite out of tune.

A rock sits grumpy, with barnacles proud,
As seaweed sways, feeling quite loud.
A crab in a bowtie struts by with glee,
In this underwater party, so wild and free.

Storms Brew

The clouds above, they start to shout,
A whale with jokes makes splashes about.
Fish in a frenzy, they swim to and fro,
As sharks jump in, putting on a show.

Bubbles like confetti float here and there,
As sea cucumbers glide without a care.
The octopus juggles, he's quite the catch,
While battling currents with a silly scratch.

Tales from the Depths

A clam tells tales of an ancient ship,
While seahorses giggle at a playful flip.
An anglerfish grins with a lantern bright,
As guppies spin tales of their wild night.

A crab's one-liner leaves all in tears,
As turtles race, forgetting their gears.
With laughter echoing through coral reefs,
These are the joys of oceanic beliefs.

A Journey into the Unknown

Down in the dark, where no one goes,
A fish spins stories, everyone knows.
With treasure maps drawn on a giant clam's back,
They swim through the muck, avoiding the snack.

An eel with a laugh gives advice quite snappy,
While cuttlefish paint, their colors all happy.
Exploring the depths, it's a comical ride,
Where every turn holds a mystery wide.

Secrets Beneath the Midnight Tide

In the dark, fish play hide and seek,
Hiding from shadows, all coy and sleek.
A crab winks, wearing a tiny crown,
While seaweed dances, all tangled down.

Starfish giggle, they've got jokes galore,
Tickled by currents, they're hard to ignore.
An octopus juggles, with eight arms strong,
Making the sea laugh all night long.

The Song of Submerged Souls

Bubbles whisper tunes that tickle the ear,
Mermaids sing songs but they drink too much beer.
A clam croons softly, taking center stage,
While the sea turtles dance, brushing off age.

Jellyfish float by, wearing hats from the shore,
Telling tall tales of what's seen on the floor.
With a splash and a flop, they disrupt the show,
Who knew this deep realm had such a funny glow?

Subtleties of the Ocean Floor

A sardine yawns, then does a little twist,
While clownfish chuckle at their frothy mist.
Seashells gossip like old friends do,
Sharing secrets in ways only they knew.

A dolphin pranks, pulling a crab's tail,
Causing a ruckus, making all turn pale.
Yet a sea cucumber just rolls its eyes,
Saying, 'Boring!' with a face full of sighs.

Where Silence Meets the Sea

Under the surface, snails tell all the news,
In hushed tones, they gossip, sharing their views.
A fish wears glasses, reading with delight,
While the sea horses vie for the best seat at night.

The anemones sway, throwing a party all day,
While the puffer fish puffs, in a funny way.
As time slips away, they all break into song,
In the depths of the sea, where they all belong.

Depths of Silent Reverie

In the stillness, fish debate,
Who can find the best bait?
A crab in thought, a shark on break,
Underwater jokes, who will make?

An octopus with colorful flair,
Dances like it hasn't a care.
A turtle slow, but wise in thought,
Snoozing while dreaming of what he's caught.

A seahorse twirls, so light and spry,
While echoing laughter flows by.
The seashells giggle, a playful bunch,
While dodging the waves that give a punch.

With bubbles popping like a cheer,
Layouts of fun, without a fear.
In this quiet ride of fun and glee,
The antics unseen, who would agree?

The Heart's Quiet Pulse

Beneath the waves, a heartbeat glows,
An unspooled yarn, where the laughter flows.
A fish in plaid, a crab in stripes,
Trading tales of hilarious gripes.

The dolphins giggle, making a splash,
As clams throw shade, quick as a flash.
Anemones wiggle in a mock dance,
While bubbles carry a playful chance.

A whale hums soft tunes, feeling grand,
As clownfish gather and form a band.
With oceanic rhythm, they spin and dive,
Together they create a party alive.

In the deep, the joy resonates,
With each punchline, laughter translates.
An echo of mirth, swirling around,
In this buoyant world, sillyness found.

Voices in the Silent Waters

Whispers of currents tell tales untold,
With each passing wave, the stories unfold.
A lobster claims he's a faraway king,
While snails chime in, 'Is it spring?'

The gurgles and giggles weave through the sea,
As critters convene for a comedy spree.
Starfish, on stage, throw their best jest,
Winking at clams who're overly blessed.

A pufferfish puffed, wearing a crown,
Boasts of the treasures he almost has found.
With bladders all laughing, bubbles arise,
This pain in sides keeps the fish mesmerized.

Tides of amusement flow without end,
Every tale shared, laughter lends.
In this mirrored vault, where giggles play,
Silent waters sing in the silliest way.

Soft Movements of the Deep Blue

In the quiet deep, jellyfish sway,
Floating about in a graceful ballet.
With arms that wave like they're in a trance,
Bubbles burst forth, creating a dance.

The sea cucumbers gossip away,
Sharing secrets with each pitter-patter play.
A starry-eyed stingray flips and twirls,
As the seashells spin, their pearls unfurl.

An eel in stripes tells fish to 'chill,'
With wisecracks that can give a thrill.
A plankton party, glow-in-the-dark,
As tiny laugh contests spark a spark.

In waves of laughter, the ocean rolls,
Where every creature brings out their souls.
Soft movements making the day feel bright,
In the shimmering dark, a comical sight.

Underneath the Veil of Night

Beneath the stars, a squirrel stumbles,
Chasing shadows, he tumbles and fumbles.
A raccoon laughs, with a twinkle in eye,
Sharing secrets, under the moonlit sky.

The crickets chirp, with a rhythm so loud,
While owls debate, in a wise, feathered crowd.
The night is a stage, where laughter ignites,
As fireflies dance in their glimmering tights.

Hushed Whispers of Infinity

In the cosmos, a cat dreams of fish,
Wishes on stars, with a twitch and a swish.
A worm sings ballads, deep in the soil,
While ants form a line, to share in the toil.

Clouds gossip lightly, in puffy white tongues,
Exchanging old tales, of their travels and runs.
A breeze joins the chorus, with a playful cheer,
As time ticks softly, bringing giggles near.

Secrets Beneath Still Waters

A frog in a pond tells stories of flies,
With each little leap, causing ripples and sighs.
The fish roll their eyes, with a flick and a grin,
As the turtles just laugh, 'Let the games begin!'

Beneath the surface, the laughter does swell,
With bubbles and splashes, they summon a spell.
The dragonflies hover, with winks and some tricks,
While the reeds sway along, sharing their quick kicks.

Currents of Calm Despair

A leaf on the water, takes life with a spin,
Waving to logs where the turtles begin.
The fish tease each other, with swirls and with plays,
While the current hums softly, through sunlit bays.

A duck quacks a joke, making ripples of cheer,
While shadows and sunlight play tag, oh so near.
The water just giggles, in its shimmering dance,
As all of the creatures join in for a chance.

Flowing Beneath the Calm

Under the water, fish wear hats,
They throw a party with party mats.
Turtles bust moves in a conga line,
While squids get tangled in the jolly twine.

The waves giggle, with bubbles they play,
As crabs do the moonwalk all night and day.
Seahorses dance to a tune so tight,
While starfish applaud, what a silly sight!

A whale on a unicycle rolls through the tide,
With dolphins cheering, they swim side by side.
Octopus juggling with popcorn galore,
Who knew the ocean had so much in store?

Mermaids sip tea from shells with a grin,
Their fairy lights flicker, inviting us in.
So come take a plunge, forget all your stress,
Join the laughter below, it's simply the best!

A Dance of Silent Spirits

In shadows of twilight where giggles ignite,
Ghosts break-dance boldly, oh what a sight!
With sheets as their outfits, they glide on the floor,
Rustling the curtains, they whisper for more.

A poltergeist serving up spooky surprise,
Bakes cookies and cakes, to our great surprise.
With frosting so bright, they delightfully cheer,
To haunt us with laughter, come join us, my dear!

Who knew the afterlife could be so much fun?
Spirits in sneakers, they twirl and they run.
Do they join in the dance, oh yes, they do try,
With ectoplasm flowing and laughter nearby.

They juggle the stars like they're balls tossed high,
As echoes of chuckles drift far through the sky.
And if you listen close, you'll hear the sweet sound,
Of giggling sprites dancing, all spinning around.

Darkness that Shimmers

In the black of the night, with a wink and a sway,
Rats hold a rave while the owls look away.
Glowworms flash dance moves beneath the old trees,
A two-step of shadows floats softly on the breeze.

The moon's a DJ, spinning tracks from the past,
While bats hang around, thinking it's quite a blast.
With whispers of mischief, they plot and they scheme,
Cat-laced conspiracies weave in a dream!

A lantern fly leads with a pulsating light,
While beetles in shades groove under the night.
The atmosphere's thick with a giggly delight,
As crickets chirp tunes to inspire the fright.

But only the brave dare to join in the game,
For darkness that shimmers is never the same.
With laughter and mischief, oh what a dark fun,
In a world full of secrets and shadows that run!

Lost in Eternity's Embrace

A clock that ticks backward, how silly it seems,
Time trips on its shoelaces, bursting our dreams.
An hourglass bubbling like soda pop fizz,
In moments of laughter, we ponder just whizz!

Eternity's feast laid out with great flair,
With sandwiches flying and soup in mid-air.
A tortoise in slippers dances on cue,
While ants on a tightrope delight in the view.

Chasing our shadows that tickle our toes,
They trip as they run, giving us quite the show.
So here we are stuck in a loop so absurd,
Silly moments stretch while we giggle unheard.

But who can complain in this timeless ballet?
With joy bubbling over, we happily stay.
For lost in the jests of forever's embrace,
We dance without worries, a whimsical space!

The Abyss' Gentle Caress

In the ocean, a tickle of glee,
A crab tried to dance with a bumblebee.
Fish wear sunglasses, oh what a sight,
They swim with a swagger, day and night.

Jellyfish giggle as they float around,
In their translucent gowns, they're quite profound.
An octopus joins with a colorful flare,
Arms waving wildly, without a care.

Seahorses playing a game of charades,
While dolphins are giggling at their escapades.
The deep is a circus, a whimsical show,
With laughter and joy, what a marvelous flow.

So dive in the funny, where the wild things roam,
In the depths of the blue, you're never alone.
With the sea as your partner, get ready to sway,
In this watery world, let laughter lead the way.

Harmonies of the Deep

Bubbles are singing a silvery tune,
While fish strum their guitars made from moon.
A shrimp on the mic, with a jazzy sway,
The undersea concert is on display.

Starfish are clapping, their arms all akimbo,
As whales croon ballads that make you limbo.
Turtles tap dance in elegant grace,
With a mermaid's wink, they set the pace.

The octopus plays tunes from years gone by,
With eight arms spinning as they inspect the sky.
Every note taken in waves of delight,
The laughter echoes through the shimmery night.

Join in the chorus, don't be shy at all,
The sea's a stage for the great and small.
With giggles and melodies that fill the space,
Dive deep into joy, let your heart race!

Voices Lost and Found

An eel tried to whisper, but slipped on a rock,
His secret was lost in a loud ticking clock.
The clams giggled softly, a pearl in surprise,
As the fish found their voices, oh what a rise!

Grouper named Larry, with wise little eyes,
Told jokes to the turtles, who burst into sighs.
They floated and bobbed, with laughter galore,
In chatty communion, they longed for more.

A walrus, quite wise, gave credit to crabs,
For making the tide rolls feel like light jabs.
They spoke of adventures, both silly and grand,
In a world made of bubbles, where laughter expands.

So listen for laughter in the bubbles of blue,
Where whispers of joy spill out just for you.
In waters enchanted, where stories are spun,
Voices are found when the light's having fun.

Dances of Light in Dark Waters

Glow-worms twirl in the twilight's embrace,
While lanternfish light up the deep, winding space.
A waltz through the shadows, both quirky and bright,
As creatures of wonder move with delight.

A glow-fish in slippers, who's ready to prance,
Invites all the sea critters to join in the dance.
They shimmy and shake, with bubbles galore,
In a frolicsome frenzy, who could ask for more?

The tide takes a turn, it's a whirlwind night,
As crabs accelerate in a comical flight.
The dance floor is swaying, the currents obey,
While seaweed does the limbo and sways all the way.

So join the procession, the splash of the fun,
In this underwater fiesta that's second to none.
With giggles and guffaws in the dim-lit embrace,
Come twirl with the fishes in a jubilant space.

Fathoms of Forgotten Dreams

Beneath the waves where fish wear hats,
A crab plays chess with two old rats.
Seaweed dances in the flow,
While turtles sing tunes from long ago.

Octopuses juggle with their eight,
And sea snails race despite their fate.
A whale tells jokes that make one groan,
In this underwater world, they're never alone.

The coral reefs giggle, not a care,
While dolphins perform like they're at the fair.
Seahorses prance in a silly parade,
As the sun sets, their antics won't fade.

So come dive deep, take a laugh with us,
In the depths where humor's never a fuss.
Forget your worries, let the sea inspire,
In this world of whimsy, you'll never tire.

The Cryptic Call of the Abyss

Down in the dark where shadows dwell,
Fish send messages, but who can tell?
A squid scribbles tales with ink so bright,
While jellyfish float, glowing with fright.

The clams all gossip, pearls in tow,
About crabs in pajamas you simply must know.
The sea cucumbers chase after a dream,
Where ice cream tides flow like a frothy stream.

A chain of barnacles sings a strange tune,
Under the watch of a grinning moon.
They tickle the sea stars, quite absurd,
Spreading joy through the depths without a word.

Join us at the dance of the wild sea floor,
Where laughter and madness are never a bore.
In this quirky realm, take a silly stance,
For the deep loves humor and a good, wacky dance.

Echoes from the Ocean's Vein

Listen closely to the bubbling sound,
A shrimp recites poetry, proudly profound.
The clowns of the sea joke as they toss,
Pearls around like they're the boss.

A pufferfish puffs up, looking so grand,
While sea turtles plan a band on the sand.
The whales join in, their voices a blend,
Singing of fish that always pretend.

Starfish play hopscotch on a sunken wreck,
While seagulls squabble over their tech.
A conch shell whispers, sharing the tales,
Of underwater shenanigans and fails.

In the ocean's heart, where the giggles flow,
Join in the dance of the ebb and the glow.
For every wave carries a chuckle or cheer,
In the laughter of currents, your worries disappear.

Shadows Cast by the Moonlit Sea

At twilight's edge where light does fade,
The fish throw a party, unafraid.
Tangled up in seaweed, they dance with glee,
While a crab narrates a tale of spree.

The moon winks down with a silvery beam,
As the tide jumps in, like a playful dream.
Starfish are stargazing, glued to the floor,
While sea urchins play a game of 'who's sore?'

The glow of a lanternfish lights up the scene,
Where mermaids in laughter giggle and preen.
Dolphins dive deep in a leap of delight,
Turning the night into pure, silly light.

So join the parade beneath the moon's glow,
In the depths of the sea where the funny things flow.
For laughter's the treasure we're all meant to find,
In shadows and currents entwined and combined.

The Quiet Symphony of Waves

Bubbles rise with a fizzy cheer,
Fish swim by with a wink, oh dear.
The crustaceans clap with their little claws,
While seaweed dances, without a pause.

A crab in a tux meets a fish in a hat,
Throwing a party, how about that!
They cha-cha on sand and sip on the foam,
It's a gala of sea creatures, far from home.

An octopus juggles shells with flair,
While starfish giggle, floating in air.
The ocean's a place where the oddballs play,
Making their music, in a watery way.

With laughter and splashes, the day glows bright,
Under the waves, all feels just right.
A raucous show, unseen by the sun,
A symphony of silliness, here's to the fun!

Mysteries Beneath the Surface

In the deep where the shadows loom,
Lurks a fish in a detective's costume.
Solving the case of the missing shell,
With a magnifying glass, he probes quite well.

A snail as a sidekick, slow but wise,
Sporting a trench coat, a clever disguise.
They question a crab, who claims he knows,
But he's too busy bragging about his pose.

Eels tell tales that cause quite a laugh,
Pretending to be the ocean's own staff.
They think the great whale is hiding a clue,
But the whale just snores, this much is true.

In bubbles and giggles, they search all around,
For mysteries lost, but giggles abound.
No treasure in sight, just friends having fun,
Beneath the blue waves, where all's come undone!

Echoes of Forgotten Souls

In the haunted reefs where the echoes play,
A ghost fish wails at the end of the day.
His gurgled songs rise to the surface,
A spectral chorus, all in great service.

The sponge on the wall, a gossiping knight,
Swears it remembers a terrible fright.
But a clam nearby, lips tightly sealed,
Claims it's just fish tales, truly concealed.

Squid in a wig dance the night away,
While soft coral tries to steal the display.
A haunted shimmy, with bumps and strange moves,
Echoes of laughter, in ghastly grooves.

With bubbles that burst, the ghost fish departs,
As sea creatures giggle, all with kind hearts.
The past may be spooky, but here's what we know,
Laughter's the light in this watery show!

Shadows Shifting Beneath Stillness

In the calm of the twilight, the shadows dance,
A sleepy old turtle lost in a trance.
He thinks it's a party, but barely can see,
As jellyfish jiggle, just one, two, three!

The sea floor is bustling with curious sights,
A clam throws a fit over late dinner bites.
While sea cucumbers lounge with a sigh,
"Do we really need more? Oh my, oh my!"

A starfish flips, showing off her moves,
While the seaweed sways, smoothly grooves.
Fish roll their eyes at the shadows' array,
"Why can't they dance like we do all day?"

But deep down, they chuckle, these quirky pals,
In their world of stillness, all giggles and gales.
Where light plays tricks, and shadows tease free,
They find their own rhythm in the deep blue sea!

Undercurrents of Longing

In the sea of desire, I float with glee,
Chasing fish that dance, oh so free!
A jellyfish tickles, it makes me laugh,
I dive for treasure, but find only trash.

A mermaid waves at me, what a sight!
She lost her comb, oh, that's not polite.
I offer her fries, from my picnic stash,
She grins and says, 'Thanks! Let's make a splash!'

The octopus juggles, it steals my breath,
With eight dancing arms, it laughs with zest.
I join the circus, we whirl and sway,
Life under the waves is a goofy ballet.

So if you feel tugged by a quirky pull,
Just dive into joy, let your heart be full.
Bubbles of laughter, they'll carry you far,
In the depths of the sea, we're all bizarre!

The Mystic Call of the Deep

I heard a voice from the murky below,
It whispered, 'Come dance, let your worries go!'
With a shake of my tail, I swam straight down,
Only to find a sea cucumber frown.

'Why so grumpy?' I asked with a grin,
He sighed, 'It's my shape—it's wearing me thin.'
I offered him cake, a delightful tease,
He turned all around, and he giggled with ease.

A crab in a top hat was strutting his stuff,
'Crustacean chic!' he announced with a huff.
We all joined the party, a seabed affair,
With conga lines forming, sea foam in the air.

Next came a fish with a dazzling flair,
Doing the twist like it just didn't care.
In the depths where the silly reigns supreme,
Life is a party—you just need to dream!

Hidden Treasures of the Soul

I dived in the depths with a quirky goal,
To find hidden treasures that spark up my soul.
A clam opened wide, and it let out a joke,
'What did the sea say? Nothing— it just spoke!'

A pile of old shoes was glittering bright,
One was a slipper, the other a flight.
I tried on the left, it sent me to dance,
With starfish and seaweed, I twirled in a trance.

Then came a dolphin with sparkles and flair,
He offered me seaweed—'Served with some care.'
We laughed till it hurt, rolling in the blue,
This treasure hunt's better with friends—yes, it's true!

So if you seek joy in the depths of your day,
Just dive with a smile—let the silliness play!
Hidden treasures await, like a giggle and cheer,
Dive in without worry, and let joy steer!

Traces of the Unknown

What's that lurking beneath the waves?
A mystery bobbing, it misbehaves!
A seaweed monster with googly eyes,
Winks at me cheerfully—what a surprise!

I asked, 'What's your name?' with a chuckle and grin,
He puffed up his chest, 'I'm Squishy McFinn!'
Together we plotted a high-seas caper,
With treasure maps drawn on an old newspaper.

A pirate passed by with a squawk and a squint,
He lost all his gold to a sneaky old shrimp.
We threw him a party with bubbles and cheer,
He danced on the deck, said, 'This is my year!'

So dive into laughter, let the currents twirl,
The unknown is funny, give it a whirl.
With characters quirky, and tales to be spun,
Beneath every surface, there's always some fun!

Ebbing Echoes of the Abyss

In the sea of lost socks, they dance,
A swirl of blue and white, not on chance.
Fish wear them like hats, it's quite a sight,
Swimming in style, they claim the night.

Oh, the jellyfish giggle at the reef,
Telling tales of deep underwater grief.
"Where did the other sock go?" they cry,
As they float with no worries, oh my my!

The crabs hold a summit on swelling foam,
Arguing if they're better off at home.
But the waves keep laughing, teasing away,
And the shells join in the fun every day.

So here's to all the lost and to the found,
In this quirky abyss, joy knows no bound.
Splashing in chaos, that's our delight,
Under the surface, life's a huge kite!

Whispers Beneath the Surface

The octopus wears glasses, what a sight,
Reading seaweed tales by the moonlight.
Starfish complain their limbs are too few,
While clams gossip secrets in a hushed hue.

"Why do turtles move so incredibly slow?"
Asked the curious shrimp with a curious glow.
"Because wisdom takes time," the turtles replied,
As they pondered the mysteries of the tide.

A dolphin skipped by with a cheeky grin,
Catching the bubbles that danced on skin.
"I'm the king of this ocean," he declared with flair,
While a clam just rolled its eyes in despair.

And so in the depths, where giggles reside,
Creatures engage in a whimsical ride.
With voices like bubbles, it's pure jubilation,
A comic ballet of aquatic sensation!

Currents of Solitude

The lonely whale sings of his missing friend,
Making echoes that twist and bend.
"Why can't I find you?" he moans with flare,
As the seaweed sways, dancing in despair.

A crab passing by offers a pie,
"A slice of fun instead of a sigh!"
"Thank you!" he croons, with a wink and a smile,
In this ocean of laughter, they stay for a while.

Anemones sway in their vibrant gowns,
As clownfish giggle, oh how they clown!
But the whale keeps searching, feeling aloof,
While a chorus of fish pulls him toward the roof.

For solitude shines in a funny old way,
With friends all around, just a giggle away.
In a sea of together, the joke's on us all,
Where even the loneliest sometimes stand tall!

The Quiet Tides of Thought

In a coral café, thoughts brew like tea,
With seahorses pondering philosophy.
"Treasures are great, but what's it all for?"
A fish exclaims, dripping wisdom from lore.

"Why dive so deep for a shiny old ring?
When you can dance close to the waves that sing?"
Echoes of laughter burst from the shell,
As a sponge hums softly to break the spell.

"Is it better to float or to swim with a plan?"
A witty old turtle says, "Be a fan!
The tide has its humor, just ride it along,
While seals were dreaming of busting a song."

So here in this depth where true thoughts ignite,
Funny comes flowing like a kite in flight.
With wisdom and laughter, we surf through the jest,
In the ocean's embrace, we all feel blessed!

Depths of Reflection

In the water's glassy sheen,
Fish ponder what they mean.
Bubbles rise with silly flair,
Like jokes whispered through the air.

Crabs wear hats at fancy balls,
While octopuses paint the walls.
A sea cucumber tells a tale,
Of the fish that tried to sail.

Seahorses prance in waltz-like streams,
Chasing after watery dreams.
With every splash and flippy flip,
They form a merry, laughing trip.

Dolphins dance, oh what a sight,
Making waves with pure delight.
Underneath, the giggles flow,
In the depths where humor grows.

Secrets Beneath the Tide

Down below where shadows play,
Crabs tell jokes and splash away.
Seaweed sways to a funny beat,
While clams share secrets, oh so sweet.

Turtles trade their favorite trends,
As starfish giggle with their friends.
Anemones tickle passing fins,
Creating laughter in their spins.

A treasure chest, a great big find,
Contains old socks and belts entwined.
Goldfish gossip with a gleeful splash,
Making waves with a cheerful clash.

Beneath the tide, the jokes abound,
In a watery world, humor's found.
With snickers and chuckles, they delight,
In the deep where all is light.

The Silent Pull of the Deep

In the silence where fish glide,
Jellyfish dream and take a ride.
With no noise, they have a ball,
Floating in their grand free fall.

Octopuses hide their pranks with glee,
Hiding things, as sly as can be.
They squirt ink, a funny sight,
And vanish in the cloak of night.

Clownfish chuckle through the reef,
Making light of their belief.
A sea urchin, in a crazy pose,
Sings a tune that no one knows.

In currents strong, the jokes unfold,
Like stories shared from days of old.
Underneath, the laughter brews,
In the quiet, where fun ensues.

Edges of the Undercurrent

At the edges where currents race,
Eels engage in a quirky chase.
A blowfish puffs, a ball of fun,
Playing peek-a-boo with everyone.

Tiny shrimp tap dance in pairs,
Lobsters crack jokes without a care.
The seashells laugh, a musical crew,
With shells that hum a tune or two.

Anemones sway, with silly grins,
As crabs boast of their wild wins.
Under waves, hilarity swells,
In the depths, where laughter dwells.

Through the eddies, cheer does flow,
With every twist, the fun will grow.
Beneath the surface, lighthearted delight,
Makes the deep a joyous sight.

The Unseen Threads of Time

In the clock's own tick-tock dance,
A squirrel steals my last cheese glance.
Threads unwind, a tangled mess,
While pets plot their own silliness.

Tea stains mark the table's edge,
As seconds leap like a wobbly hedge.
Time giggles at all our schemes,
As shoelaces tangle into dreams.

With every laugh and silly jest,
We find our place, we do our best.
The past chuckles, so cheeky and spry,
While future plans just wave goodbye.

So let us dance on life's fine line,
With wit and jokes that intertwine.
For every moment, though it's brief,
Deserves a chuckle, not just grief.

Quietude in the Underworld

In caverns deep where shadows play,
A troll sings loudly, quite the ballet.
His audience? Bats in a zest,
Who laugh at his dance, well, they're impressed!

A ghost pops up for ghostly jokes,
But skeletons laugh like clumsy folks.
With rattling bones and echoes wide,
They sway to the rhythm of the guide.

Down here where the stones arise,
We wear our best unearthly ties.
A goblin serves tea with bats in flight,
What a show for a spooky night!

In quietude beneath the ground,
The merry sounds of mischief abound.
Who knew the underworld could bring,
Such joy and tales that make hearts sing?

The Subtle Cradle of the Ocean

Bubbles rise like balloons in fear,
As fish throw parties without any cheer.
The seaweed sways in a dizzy spin,
While crabs do the cha-cha with a fin!

An octopus juggles with shells galore,
Sardines swim in for an encore.
They giggle and twirl in watery peace,
Finding treasures, their worries cease.

The waves hum tunes, a soft serenade,
While starfish claim their sunbathing grade.
Seahorses gossip 'bout the latest trend,
In this cradle, laughter has no end.

So join this circus in blue delight,
Where the finned folk laugh and leap in flight.
The ocean's charm is a joyful spree,
In the cradle of waves, it's all silly glee!

Murmurs of the Moonlit Tide

Under the moon, where surfers glide,
The sea whispers secrets, full of pride.
A seal flips somersaults, makes a splash,
While gulls squawk loudly, raucous and brash.

The tide rolls in with a giggly swoosh,
And mermaids join like a glittery roosh.
They twirl and swirl in silver beads,
Planting jokes like underwater seeds.

With waves that chuckle, soft and round,
Crabs tap their claws; what a funny sound!
The night is bright with mischievous stars,
As jellyfish dance near imaginary cars.

So listen close, beneath the bright gleam,
The water's laughter flows like a dream.
In moonlit tides, with friends all around,
The murmurs of joy in waves abound.

Tidal Whispers of the Soul

In the ocean's grand ballet, fish wear hats,
Dancing to the seaweed's funky beats.
A clam rapped and the krill clapped,
Shells twinkling like disco treats.

Bubbles whisper silly dreams,
Seahorses giggle, bobbing about.
The sandy floor is a stage, it seems,
Where starfish try out their best pout.

Octopuses play hide and seek,
Squirting ink at the jokes they tell.
But behind those smiles, they're rather meek,
Just hoping not to slip and yell!

In this world of watery mirth,
Where laughter flows like the tide.
Every splash brings another birth,
Of giggles from the ocean wide.

Fantasies Beneath the Blue

Under the waves, a party's planned,
Crabs juggling under bright seashells.
Mermaids crafting candy, so grand,
While sharks throw in silly spells.

A narwhal dons a rainbow wig,
Flipping through bubbles like a pro.
The fish all laugh at the sight so big,
As they twirl in a wiggle-show.

Turtles race in slow-motion sprints,
Wearing sunglasses to catch a glance.
A dolphin slips and shows its flints,
As all join in a slippery dance.

Among these dreams, so sweet and bright,
Laughter echoes through the foam.
In the depths, what a comical sight,
Where silliness feels like home.

The Glistening Silence of Depths

In the stillness, the fish all sing,
Turtle concerts, the highlight, no doubt.
A wink from a stingray is the real king,
While snails spin jokes, roundabout.

The sea cucumbers crack little puns,
With faces that brighten the gloom.
As jellyfish flash, everyone runs,
To dance in the glittering room.

A rolling wave gives a hearty cheer,
As octopus plays 'Hide the Ink'.
Giggling bubbles swish in the sphere,
Making the shyest of fish rethink.

Laughter echoes in watery rows,
As seababies tumble with glee.
In the depths, where joy freely flows,
Every gurgle is pure jubilee.

Secrets of the Water's Veil

Behind the veils of the liquid blue,
Clams drop secrets that giggle and gleam.
Seahorses sip on a drink or two,
Flirting with bubbles, living the dream.

A whale tells tales with a splashy grin,
While seaweed sways to the rhythm divine.
To otters and dolphins, the laughs begin,
As they chase their fins through briny wine.

The deep keeps secrets, oh so sly,
Creatures wearing sunglasses in sync.
With each little wave, you can't deny,
The humor that fills every wink and blink.

So join the frolic and splash about,
For who knows what lies in sea's embrace?
With laughter's echo and no doubt,
Together, we'll paint the ocean's face.

Glimmers of Forgotten Reflections

In a pond where frogs start to sing,
A lost shoe does a jig, what joy it can bring.
The fish in tuxedos swim with delight,
While turtles cheer on in their slow, quirky flight.

Mice on tiny rafts float by the shore,
Nibbling on cheese, they always want more.
With each little splash and awkward dive,
Even the duck seems to laugh and thrive.

Bubbles of laughter burst in the air,
As quacking ducks gossip and gossip with flair.
Who knew the water could be a dance floor?
For all of its secrets, there's always much more.

So if you seek joy in the most silly ways,
Jump in the puddles and brighten your days.
'Cause within every splash, every wiggle and sway,
Lies a giggle, a grin, and sunshine to play.

The Peace Beneath the Turbulence

In the wake of a cannonball's splashy spree,
A grandpa recites tales as grand as the sea.
Kids dart around like fish on a quest,
All giggles and bubbles, they shine at their best.

A crab wearing glasses studies the shore,
While seagulls discuss the best snacks to score.
Nature's a comedy, dressed in wild hues,
Each wave a punchline as laughter ensues.

Under the chaos, a calm elf resides,
With a tiny umbrella, she tries to hide.
While splashes abound and the chaos ignites,
She sips on her tea, with a smirk that excites.

Between giggles and splashes, the joy takes flight,
In the midst of the uproar, there's peace in the light.
The world may be wild, but in folly we find,
A laughter-filled harmony, wondrous and kind.

Beneath Calm Waters

Beneath the glassy surface, so calm and so bright,
The fishes throw parties, oh what a sight!
They boogie in circles, all fins in a whirl,
While the eel plays guitar, it's a magical twirl.

A snail with a top hat takes center stage,
With moves that could rival the best of a page.
Tadpoles in tuxedos are ready to groove,
As they wiggle and jive, they've all found their move.

A bubblegum jellyfish floats with a grin,
Just in time to witness the fun about to begin.
Each creature joins in, under the moon's glowing posters,
In a comedy of nature, they're all perfect roasters.

So when you look down, don't just see the blue,
There's a world under there, of silliness too.
The laughter resounds, a harmony so true,
Where calm waters ripple with humor anew.

Stories Linger

At twilight, the waters start to tell tales,
Of daring fish missions and turtle-scale fails.
A crab tells a secret that makes lobsters chuckle,
While the seaweed giggles, it gives off a shuffle.

Each splash is a chapter, each wave a new line,
Where jellyfish recount how they danced with a swine.
In the dusk, the waters are filled with fairy lights,
While clam shells applaud the comedic delights.

The octopus juggles, but forgets his last trick,
And all of the onlookers respond with a click.
As laughter erupts from the depths of the sea,
The echoes of joy drift to shores in pure glee.

In these moments of mirth, we find what makes us whole,
A connection through stories, their impact our goal.
So gather 'round tightly, let each tale unfold,
For in every adventure, there's a laugh to be told.

The Liquid Canvas of Thought

In the vibrant splash of a paint-filled stream,
Thoughts swirl like colors, in a whimsical dream.
A goldfish with glasses sketches a scene,
Where the ducks do ballet, oh what can it mean?

In rippling laughter, the water's a muse,
As frogs in berets each choose their own views.
With a brush made of seaweed and bubbles for ink,
They create a ruckus as they both swim and think.

The canvas evolves with each splatter and dash,
As minnows join in for a vibrant splash.
Colors unite in a joyful parade,
Creating a masterpiece that cannot quite fade.

So dip in your toes, and let worries drift,
For art in the water is life's greatest gift.
Within every splash, a new story begins,
Funny and bright, where joy truly wins.

Dreams Adrift in Unseen Currents

Bubbles bounce, a fish in a hat,
Dreams float by like a plump acrobat.
A seaweed dance, the jellies giggle,
Fishy laughter, what a wiggly wiggle!

Crabs tell tales of pirates bold,
While mermaids sleep, all strung in gold.
A clam sings softly, a tune so bright,
Making the octopus lose its sight!

Seashells gossip on sandy shores,
Telling more jokes than a sea lion roars.
A wave of chuckles, a tidal tease,
Tickling the fins of the sea with ease!

In this watery funhouse, oh what a sight,
Dreams have wings, taking off in flight.
Every wave crashes with a silly dip,
Join the party, don't let it slip!

Shadows That Swim

Under the surface, where shadows tangle,
Fish with sunglasses do a cool jangle.
They flip and they flop, with swagger and style,
Making the deep end feel like a mile!

A wiggly worm pulls a dance so neat,
While clams choose partners, shuffling their feet.
A flounder flat out forgets its moves,
As laughter erupts, the whole ocean grooves!

Eels make jokes, all twisted and fun,
While crabs do the hustle, oh what a run!
The shadows swim with laughter in tow,
Creating a party where sea creatures glow!

Octopuses giggle, their tentacles flail,
Making a splash, drawing a colorful trail.
In the cool water where laughter takes flight,
All shadows mingle, oh what a sight!

The Beneath of Light

Beneath the shimmers, where fishy tales dwell,
Anemones dance, casting a spell.
Bright colors twirl, like a carnival ride,
Every bubble bursting with laughter inside!

Crabby comedians crack up the place,
As starfish join in, all smiles on their face.
With every flicker of the peeping light,
Even the rocks join with sheer delight!

The whispers of waters are jokes on the flow,
Where nothing is serious, just letting it go.
A playful current tickles a sea cucumber,
As seahorses giggle, losing their slumber!

In the glow of the moon, waves ripple and joke,
Creating a circus, as bright as smoke.
A soft wave laughs, in the depths of the night,
Bringing the magic, the beneath of light!

Whispers in the Current

Whispers bubble like fizzy soda,
Turtles doze off in a wobbly moda.
A playful dolphin spins tales so tall,
In the water's hum, we hear it all!

Giggling fish trade gossip galore,
While sea urchins roll, laughing on the floor.
Crustacean comedians crack one-liners quick,
Making shells shake with a hilarious kick!

A sneaky sea snake tells tales of the great,
As corals chime in, "Don't be late!"
Every wave holds a joke in its swell,
In the current's embrace, all creatures yell!

The laughter cascades, as bubbles pop,
Creating a ruckus, stop and shop!
Where laughter flows freely, joy shines bold,
In the gentle waves, happy stories unfold!

Shadows in the Stillness

In a pond where the frogs like to croak,
A fish spun around to tell a joke.
"Why did the turtle cross the street?"
He quipped with a grin, oh what a feat!

The shadows danced, a quirky ballet,
As tadpoles giggled, brightening the day.
A duck waddled in, quacking with cheer,
Said, "I'm just here for the laughs, never fear!"

The minnows swirled in a comical whirl,
While dragonflies zipped, causing a twirl.
"Oh my," sighed the old catfish with a smirk,
"Can't they see I'm too cool for this work?"

But all in the stillness, the laughter did rise,
With shadows to play tricks upon their wise eyes.
As they splashed and they played in the afternoon sun,
The water, it chuckled, as they all had fun!

Currents of the Unseen

In the deep where the currents do weave,
Swam a slow snail with dreams up his sleeve.
He pondered and plotted how fast he could glide,
Yet all of his plans took a turn for the ride!

A crab strutted by with a sideways jig,
"Hey there, my friend, you look rather big!
Why don't you join me in a game of tag?"
The snail just sighed, "I'm too slow, oh a drag!"

The seaweed swayed to an unseen beat,
With fish in sunglasses, they danced to the heat.
"Oh, to be swift!" the poor snail did crave,
Yet here in the current, he learned how to wave!

With bubbles that giggled and sparkles that twinkled,
He watched as a starfish often just crinkled.
"Life's not about speed, it's about having fun!"
As currents of laughter beneath the waves run!

Waves of Forgotten Dreams

In the surf, where the seagulls complain,
A lobster baked in a sunbeam, quite insane.
He dreamed of being a strong king so grand,
Yet ended up stuck in the soft, golden sand!

"Hey, Mr. Clam, lend me your pearly shell,
I need a cool crown, can't you tell?"
The clam just flipped, "You look fine as you are,
With dreams in the sea, you'll go very far!"

An octopus popped up, all arms in a twist,
"I might have a job where nobody missed!
You'll be my assistant, just look at my charms,
Together we'll sell seaweed in bulk at the farms!"

But dreaming of kings and grand ocean fame,
The lobster just smiled, 'Tis a whimsical game.
For all of the waves and the sun's golden beams,
He learned laughter is best, far beyond all his dreams!

Lurking Secrets of the Ocean

Beneath the waves in a dark, murky zone,
A fish named McFinn claimed he was alone.
He lurked and he darted, but oh what a prank,
His secrets were funny, not grand like he spanked!

"I'm a deep-sea detective!" he'd say with a wink,
"Searching for treasures, come drink from my sink!"
A turtle nearby scoffed from his place,
"Your 'treasures' are just bits of seaweed and lace!"

With a flip and a wiggle he swam with delight,
"Underwater antics are quite the good sight!
We find hidden treasures of laughter and cheer,
Like a crab on a tricycle, let's give it a steer!"

In laughter they rolled, oh such jovial fun,
As bubbles popped up whilst the ocean did run.
Secrets of humor in currents did swirl,
For even the sea has its whimsical pearl!

The Enigmatic Song of Shadows

In a world where shadows prance,
They wear hats and do a dance.
Lurking quietly, they tease a joke,
While the moonlight starts to poke.

Whispering secrets in the night,
They giggle, causing quite the fright.
Chasing fireflies, they leap and swirl,
Unruly spirits in a twirly whirl.

When a clock strikes, they freeze like stone,
Then burst out laughing with a tone.
A game of tag, they never win,
Just shadows playing with a grin.

So if you see them, don't be shy,
Dance with them, and let your heart fly.
For in their midst, joy's alive,
In this game, we'll all survive.

Dreams Flowing in the Abyss

In a land where dreams collect,
With fish who knit and sprinkle wrecks,
Stars roll by like silly marbles,
Rolling laughter, no time to squabble.

A jellyfish sings an off-key tune,
While octopuses dance 'neath the moon.
Whales in bow ties swim right past,
Chasing bubbles, what a blast!

Mermaids gather for tea at dusk,
Sipping seaweed, oh what a husk!
Their tales of adventure, you'll adore,
As they giggle and beg for more.

So join the party down below,
Where laughter and giggles freely flow.
In the depths, where dreams can soar,
Every moment holds a quirky encore.

When Stars Meet the Sea

Dancing lights above the tide,
Stars slip and slide with a grin wide.
Waves chuckle as they crash and play,
"Oh look! A star fish!" they laugh all day.

Galaxies wiggle, splash around,
Merry melodies in the sound.
Bright comets hide in seaweed beds,
Winking brightly, in sparkly threads.

When night falls, the sea takes flight,
In this wacky, whimsical sight.
Mariners chuckle, "Let's glide and twirl,"
As the ocean waves with a twist and whirl.

For in the meeting of sky and foam,
Laughter echoes, calling us home.
A spark, a flicker, a giggle here,
Under the stars, let's shed your fear.

Sirens of the Deepest Blue

In the depths where giggles reign,
Sirens swim, avoiding the mundane.
With hair like kelp and laughs like waves,
They pull you in, in quirky caves.

"Come dance with us!" they sing with glee,
"I'll trade you secrets if you see!"
They sprinkle salt on every word,
To make their gossip more absurd.

When sailors stumble to their song,
They're tickled pink, they join along.
What was a quest now turns to fun,
As sea meets sky, they laugh and run.

So heed the call of giddy chimes,
Leave your worries and silly crimes.
In the laughter of the ocean's crew,
Find your joy, it's waiting for you.

Mysterious Depths of Emotion

In the ocean of feelings, I float with a grin,
Chatting with mermaids, I challenge them to spin.
They ask me for secrets, but I'm shy as a clam,
Yet I do a cartwheel and say, "Here I am!"

Waves tickle my toes, like old friends at play,
A jellyfish jokes, 'You should join in today!'
But I twirl with a shrimp, as the dolphins declare,
'He's the king of this sea, with a saltwater flair!'

Barnacles laugh as they cling to a rock,
Admiring my moves, who knew I could shock?
I dance with the seaweed, it sways and it bends,
In this wacky abyss, I've found so many friends!

So dive deep with me in this curious zone,
Where laughter keeps bubbling, and madness is grown.
The ocean's a circus, my heart is its clown,
In these whimsical depths, I shall never frown!

Beneath the Stillness

Beneath the calm surface, a party is grand,
With fish in tuxedos, they groove on the sand.
A whale plays the trumpet, a crab keeps the beat,
While sea cucumbers think they're way too elite!

The turtles are racing, in slow-motion style,
While seahorses giggle with a cheeky smile.
A starfish brings snacks, it's all quite a snack,
And even the octopus joins in for the smack!

Anemones whisper, 'What's that joke you tell?'
A pufferfish bursts out, saying, "All is swell!"
I laugh till I wobble, oh, this mermaid's delight,
In the stillness below, with my friends, all is right!

So join in the fun, in this undersea laugh,
With friends from the depths, we're a whimsical staff.
No worries or cares, just a splash and a cheer,
We dance in the darkness, and we bring the good cheer!

Veils of the Midnight Sea

In shadows of black, where the lanternfish gleam,
I navigate currents, like I'm in a dream.
With a whale's whoopee cushion, I float through the night,

Sharing giggles with glowworms, what a weird sight!

The octopus winks with a wide, silly grin,
While jellyfish juggle, and fish sport a fin.
A murky abyss, but there's fun in the dark,
Where creatures have parties, igniting the spark!

Dolphins play charades, with bubbles as clues,
And sea urchins crack jokes, delivering news.
The crab with the top hat thinks he's quite the chap,
While I snicker and sink in my undersea nap!

So let's paint the night with our laughter and glee,
In the veils of the ocean, where we all feel free.
No worries to cling to, just joy in the tide,
In this midnight ballet, where we all can glide!

Constellations of the Deep Blue

In the cosmos of ocean, where starlights are waves,
I sail with my fish friends, all in colored braves.
A starry-eyed angler shows off his bright bait,
While a dolphin reads fortunes, claiming it's fate!

Beneath splashes of laughter, the squids hold a toast,
To the greatest of moments, they brag and they boast.
A clam does a handstand, oh what a sight,
In this disco of bubbles, we twirl with delight!

The urchins provide glam, with glittering style,
Crabs strut like models, just catwalk a mile.
A lobster in shades declares, "I'm the prime!"
While sea turtles chime in with buttery rhymes.

So chart out your course, in this fun-filled sea,
With constellations of laughter, wild and carefree.
In layers of water, where whims dance and play,
We shine through the depths, in our own quirky way!

The Depths' Embrace

In the ocean's cozy grip,
Fish wear sunglasses, take a trip.
Jellyfish dance, so carefree,
They've got moves we'd all agree.

Crabs hold parties, shellfish too,
With seaweed snacks and ocean brew.
Laughter bubbles, what a scene,
Even turtles join the routine.

Octopus dons a polka dot tie,
Eats his pasta while passing by.
The coral choir sings with flair,
Sea cucumbers—quite debonair!

At the dawn, the sea's awake,
Mermaids bake with a sea salt flake.
Where the funny fishes swim and glide,
In the depths, joy cannot hide!

Beneath the Surface

A clam complains of life's slow pace,
While seahorses compete in a race.
Starfish chill on a sandy throne,
Making sandcastles all alone.

The dolphin jokes, "I'm quite the catch,"
As octopuses try to sketch.
Each wave brings chuckles, no distress,
A clownfish painted to impress.

The seaweed sways, a silly dance,
While shrimp get lost in a trance.
The great abyss, a stage so bright,
Underwater laughs bring pure delight.

As bubbles rise, they burst with glee,
In the depths, there's always a spree.
Beneath the waves, surprise awaits,
With each splash, excitement creates!

A Tale Unfolds

Once a fish with a floppy fin,
Decided it was time to begin.
He flipped and flopped with all his might,
Bumping into a jellyfish sprite.

Together they swam, quite the pair,
Claiming the depths as their fair share.
With every turn, they'd joke and tease,
'Twas the best of times, if you please!

A whale decided to come join the fun,
Said, "Laughter's a sport, let's all run!"
But in his haste, he caused a splash,
And all their games turned into a crash.

They tumbled around, in giggles entwined,
Playing tag with the ocean defined.
The tale unfolds in waves of joy,
With fishy friends, no room for coy.

The Flowing Silence

Bubbles rise, what a quiet scheme,
Whales and fishes glide like a dream.
In the silence where laughs are born,
Anemones dance to the silent horn.

A hermit crab with an empty shell,
Wants to host a party: "Oh, what the hell!"
He decorates with bits of bright trash,
And invites the sea over for a bash!

With each surprise, a chuckle erupts,
Even a pufferfish joins and erupts.
They feast on plankton, oh such delight,
In their flowing silence, the mood's just right.

Dancing with currents, a theatrical play,
Underwater antics brighten the day.
Amidst the calm, joy sneaks in,
In this quiet world, we giggle and grin!

Beneath Waves, the Heart Speaks

When tides rise high, emotions flow,
An otter juggles snails in a show.
He slips and slides, oh what a sight,
As sea creatures roar with pure delight.

A mermaid strums on a seashell harp,
Singing tales of the ocean's heart, so sharp.
With every note, the water sways,
Creating laughter in merry arrays.

Yet deep down, where shadows play,
A crab makes jokes about the day.
"I'm just pinching, not causing any strife,"
His funny quips bring joy to life.

In this ocean of whimsy, there's no defeat,
Beneath waves where hearts dance and meet.
With humor entwined in every sweep,
The ocean sings while the world takes a leap!

www.ingramcontent.com/pod-product-compliance
Lightning Source LLC
Chambersburg PA
CBHW062111280426
43661CB00086B/492